Table of Contents

Vegetable Production In Greenhouses

Barry Nadel

General Concepts

The Mini Professional Greenhouse (MPG) is equipped with a computer program that controls all the climatic conditions automatically for the grower. There are a series of icons in your app that allows you to choose the growing protocol. There are seven general protocols. It is highly recommended that you grow only the plants in one particular group at a time so that growing conditions don't conflict and cause the computer to not provide the proper growing environment.

Alternative to Organics

Alternative to Organics (ATO) is a new concept in producing crops that are safe for human consumption. Organically grown crops are defined as food[1] produced by methods that observe with the principles of organic farming[2]. The regulations vary worldwide. Generally, organic farming strives to cycle resources, promote ecological balance, restrict the use of synthetic pesticides, and reserve biodiversity[3]. Most organizations regulating organic products restrict the use of certain pesticides[4] and fertilizers[5] in farming. Many countries require that the plant be connected to the soil to be labeled organic. In general, organic foods are also usually not processed using irradiation[6], industrial solvents or synthetic food additives[7].

The concept of ATO was created to answer a number of problems that organic growing doesn't deal with. Most people believe that organic crops are safer to eat than non-organic crops. However, regulations for organic growing miss several important safety features. They are:

1. Don't require testing the water used in irrigation for pollutants of all sorts (pesticides, fertilizers, and heavy metals).
2. Don't require testing of the soil for pollutants of all sorts (pesticides, fertilizers, and heavy metals).
3. Don't require the treatment of the runoff water.

---

1. https://en.wikipedia.org/wiki/Food

2. https://en.wikipedia.org/wiki/Organic_farming

3. https://en.wikipedia.org/wiki/Biodiversity

4. https://en.wikipedia.org/wiki/Pesticide

5. https://en.wikipedia.org/wiki/Fertilizer

6. https://en.wikipedia.org/wiki/Irradiation

7. https://en.wikipedia.org/wiki/Food_additives

The concept of ATO is to ensure that the crops you grow are not polluted by the soil or water. What is the use of organically grown crops that were produced on polluted soil or irrigated with contaminated water?

A crop grown under ATO regulations differs from organic in the following manner.

1. Organic doesn't allow the use of artificial media.

2. Organic is concerned with the use of pesticides and other poisons.

3. ATO emphasizes ecologically safe pesticides, and demands careful use of all pesticides, including protecting the sprayer (with proper protective gear) and maintaining the proper interval of time from the employment of the pesticide before consumption.

4. ATO considers the overall quality of the water for human consumption, not only pesticides, but heavy metals, sewage and poisons from any source.

5. ATO crops will be grown in soil/media that are free of sewage, poisons of all types and free of heavy metal toxicity.

Synthetic vs Organic fertilizers

In popular literature and especially on the internet where articles are written without peer evaluation, many misconceptions are passed around. However, if you read the scientific papers on the subjects, you find that the main problem with modern agriculture isn't the technologies, but human abuse.

The problem with 'synthetic fertilizers' they break down slower in nature and are overused by farmers. The various components of the fertilizer leak into the ground water and from there spread throughout the ecosystem.

Another area of misconception is Genetically Modified Organisms (GMOs). There is no significant scientific research to substantiate the "evils of Genetically Modified Organisms". There are no reports of GMO foods causing damage to humans or animals. What does happen frequently is misuse of herbicides. Many of the GMO crops have resistance to the herbicide Roundup. Unfortunately, many farmers over-spray, keeping their fields clean of weeds and thus increasing their yields. However, this abuse of herbicide leaves trace amounts in the food and pollutes ground water.

Toxicological research found the following results: "These results demonstrate that dsRNA for insect control does not produce adverse health effects in mammals at oral doses millions to billions of times higher than anticipated human exposures and therefore poses negligible risk to mammals (Petrick, et al. 2016).

People opposed to GMOs speak of the evils they create as if they will slowly kill you. It would be political suicide to attack farmers. What needs to be done is simple. All crops need to be tested for pesticides. If a farmer's crop shows higher levels of pesticides than permitted by health authorities, then it must be destroyed.

There is no better way to control misuse than to hit the offender in the pocketbook. The fear of losing one's livelihood will stop the abuse. Crops should be analyzed for pesticides and if above the approved amounts the crop should be destroyed.

The same situation exists with synthetic fertilizer. Once again, the main problem is overuse. Many farmers "pump" their crops with nitrogen to increase size so they will get better prices. The solution is not to outlaw the fertilizer, but to regulate its use.

ATO proposes that all greenhouses treat their runoff water before it is returned into the ecosystem. Treatment ponds need to be made and aquatic plants should be grown that are efficient at removing nitrogen, phosphates, and potassium from the water. The water should be tested and not allowed to be release back into the ecosystem until approval by health authorities.

Removing soil Contaminates

The old method of removing soil contaminates was to physically remove the contaminated soil. Mushrooms, bacteria and growing plants can help contain or reduce heavy metal pollution. This is often called phytoremediation (EPA, 1988). It has the advantage of relatively low cost and wide public acceptance (Schnoor, 1997). Trees and grass are grown around the contaminated area to reduce erosion. This method confines the pollutant and greatly reduces its spread to non-contaminated soils.

Phytoextraction is a method of growing plants on contaminated soils that can remove heavy metals from soils by absorbing them into their tissues. When the crop is finished growing, it is harvested, dried and burned. The heavy metals can be found in the ash. Depending on the amount of pollutants, anywhere from grams to kilos can be recovered from a plot of $1000m^2$.

Rhizofiltration is another method. In this method roots extract heavy metals. In an experiment employing sunflower on floating rafts removed radioactive metals from water in ponds at Chernobyl (EPA 2000) and clean up a uranium plant in Ohio.

Brazil has abandoned gold mines leaking mercury and other heavy metals into the soil and water. Mercury is one of the most toxic of heavy metals and readily passed along in the food change. Grass growing on contaminated soil and eaten by cows pass the mercury onto us. Brazilian farmers now grow maize and canola in those areas. Both species absorb gold and mercury. Up to a kilogram/ hectare of gold can be extracted from the plants.

Experiments with mustard greens removed 45% of the excess lead from a yard in Boston, to improve the safety of children who play there. In

Trenton, New Jersey, pumpkin vines were employed to clean up an old factory. The British used Alpine pennycress to help clean up abandoned mines.

Yellow poplars can convert a toxic form of mercury to a more benign form.

Water ferns, blue sheep fescue and members of the cabbage family absorb lead from polluted water sources and soil. Smooth water hyssop takes up copper and mercury. One of the superstars is water hyacinths. They absorb mercury, lead, cadmium, zinc, cesium, strontium-90, uranium and various pesticides. Sunflowers can also remove a wide range of compounds –uranium and strontium-90 from radioactive sites, but also cesium, methyl bromide, zinc and copper. Bladder campion accumulates zinc and copper, while Indian mustard greens concentrate selenium, Sulphur, lead, chromium, cadmium, nickel, zinc, and copper.

Perhaps the most magnificent hyper-accumulator, is the willow tree, Salix viminalis. Willow absorbs copper, zinc, cadmium, selenium, silver, chromium, uranium, petrochemicals and many others. Also, once its bio-mass has concentrated the heavy metals, it can be harvested and used.

Phytoremediation is restricted by the ability of specific plants t grow in specific contaminated areas, and should not be an invasive species. For example, the use of kudzu in the American South which took over the landscape. Plants can only remove toxins as deep as their roots, so the technique might not solve groundwater contamination.

Growing Groups

These are groupings of plants that organic growers find that grow well together.

1. Solanaceae Tomato, pepper, eggplants, asparagus, coriander, dill, mint, thyme, basil, oregano, okra, and lettuce.

1. Cucurbits

cucumbers, summer squash, winter squash, mini watermelons, green onion, melons. parsley, kohlrabi, peas, onions.

1. Brassica

Broccoli, cauliflower, kale, Brussels sprout, Swiss Chard, Chinese cabbage, turnip, mustard, celery, spinach, peas, lettuce, parsley.

1. Root crops

Beets, carrots, kohlrabi, basil, oregano, mint, lettuce, parsley, rutabaga, daikon, radish, parsnip, scallion, celery, horse radish.

1. Herbs and Spices

Oregano, basil, parsley, coriander, thyme, dill, mint, green onion, scallion, mustard, peppermint.

1. Legumes

Peas, black eyed beans, lima beans, kidney beans, navy beans, mung beans, black beans, yard long beans, cucumber, radish, strawberry

1. Cannabis, basil, beans, garlic, and mint.

Organic Pesticides

Herbicides:

In recent years, a number of organic herbicides are for sale. They are all contact herbicides and have no systemic effect. Take care when spraying because they will also burn your crops. They are based on:

20% acetic acid

5% citric acid

55% d-limonene

50% clove oil

45% clove oil + 45% cinnamon oil and

50% lemongrass oil.

Eugenol

2-Phenethyl Propionate

Sodium Lauryl Sulfate

Ammonium Nonanoate

Pelargonic Acid + Fatty Acids

These organic products may be effective in controlling weeds, but have limitations. These organic herbicides can kill weeds that have emerged from the soil. They have no residual activity on weeds emerging afterwards. These herbicides can burn back the tops of perennial weeds, perennial weeds recover quickly.

These organic products are effective in controlling weeds when the weeds are small but are less effective on older plants. In a recent study

(Lanini) found that weeds in the cotyledon or first true leaf stage were more susceptible to organic control than older weeds. These organic herbicides work much better when the temperature is above 24°C. Improve the effectiveness of organic herbicides, by thoroughly spraying to a point where the herbicide is running off plant leaf surface.

A classic organic herbicide is made in the following way. Table salt 1 cup, vinegar 5% two cups and four liters of water. If a higher percent of vinegar is available it will kill the weeds faster

Insecticides

Bordeaux Mix,

Copper sulfate and lime mixed in water is good against snails and slugs.

Neem

This natural plant extract has been used in India from ancient times. Neem oil is a powerful, all-natural plant extract for warding off pests. In fact, neem juice is the most powerful natural pesticide on the planet, holding over 50 natural insecticides. You can use this extremely bitter tree leaf to make a natural pesticide spray.

Neem oil spray is made by adding 1/2 an ounce of high-quality organic neem oil and ½ teaspoon of a mild organic liquid soap to two quarts of warm water. Stir slowly. It should be use immediately.

Salt Spray

For treating plants infested with spider mites, mix two tablespoons of Himalayan Crystal Salt[1] into one gallon of warm water and spray on infected areas.

Mineral Oil

Mix 10-30 ml of high-grade oil with one liter of water. Mix thoroughly Stir and add to spray bottle. This organic pesticide works well for dehydrating insects and their eggs.

Citrus Oil and Cayenne Pepper

---

1. http://www.globalhealingcenter.com/natural-health/himalayan-crystal-salt-benefits/

This mixture works well on ants. Mix 10 drops of citrus essential oil with one teaspoon cayenne pepper and 1 cup of warm water. Mix well and spray the affected areas.

Soap, Orange Citrus Oil, and Water

To make this natural pesticide, simply mix three tablespoons of liquid Organic Castile soap with 1 ounce of orange oil to one gallon of water. Shake well. This is an especially effective treatment against slugs and can be sprayed directly on ants and roaches.

Eucalyptus Oil

A great natural pesticide for flies, bees, and wasps. Simply sprinkle a few drops of eucalyptus oil where the insects are found. They will all be gone before you know it.

Onion and Garlic Spray

Mince one organic clove of garlic and one medium sized organic onion. Add to a quart of water. Wait one hour and then add one teaspoon of cayenne pepper and one tablespoon of liquid soap to the mix. This organic spray will hold its potency for one week if stored in the refrigerator.

Chrysanthemum Flower Tea

These flowers hold a powerful plant chemical component called pyrethrum. This substance invades the nervous system of insects, rendering them immobile. You can make your own spray by boiling 100 grams of dried flowers into 1 liter of water. Boil dried flowers in water for twenty minutes. Strain, cool, and pour into a spray bottle. Can be stored for up to two months. You can also add some organic neem oil to enhance the effectiveness.

Tobacco Spray

Just as tobacco is hazardous to humans, tobacco spray was once a commonly used pesticide for killing pests, caterpillars, and aphids. Mix one cup of organic tobacco (preferably a brand that is organic and all-natural) into one gallon of water. Allow the mixture to set overnight. After 24-hours, the mix should have a light brown color. If it is very dark, add more water. This mix can be used on most plants, except those in the solanaceous family (tomatoes, peppers, eggplants, etc.)

Chile Pepper / Diatomaceous Earth

Grind two handfuls of dry chilies into a fine powder and mix with 1 cup of Diatomaceous earth. Add to 2 liters of water and let set overnight. Shake well before applying.

False Codling Moth (CFM) *Thaumatotibia leucotreta* attacks a large variety of fruits and vegetables. There is an excellent biological control which employs the use of a pathogenic virus called *Cryptophlebia leucotreta* granulovirus (CrleGV). It has been reported in Africa to attack hot chile peppers. Follow instructions of locally produced virus.

Organic Fungicides

Baking Soda: 4 teaspoons of Baking Soda, 1 teaspoon of mild liquid soap added to four liters of water.

Copper solutions

Bordeaux Mix" 450 gm lime into 1 gallon of water and let it stand for at least two hours. This allows you to make a quick solution of **Bordeaux**. Fill a bucket with 2 gallons water and add 1 quart of the copper solution.

Various copper compounds and their use (Table 1)

Table   1   Organic   Copper   Fungicides

Active ingredient	Metallic copper equivalent	gm/1000m2 Broccoli[**]	gm/1000m2 Lettuce	gm/1000m2 Squash[***]	gm/1000m2 Tomato[#]	REI[^]	PHI[*]
24% copper oxychloride + 21% copper hydroxide	28%	85	199	142	199	48hr	0 day
98% basic copper sulfate	53%	341	341	227	284	24hr	0 day
58% copper salts of fatty and rosin acids	5.14%	88ml	352 ml	352ml	352ml	12hr	0 day
77% copper hydroxide	50%	227	----	341	454	24hr	0 day
19.8% copper sulfate pentahydrate	5%	192ml	----	192ml	240ml	48hr	0 day
10% copper octanoate	180%	950ml	950 ml	950ml	950ml	4hr	0 day
84% cuprous oxide	75%	142	142	142	284	24hr	0 day
77% copper hydroxide	50%	114	114	142	227	24hr	1 day
^Restricted Entry Interval							
*Pre-Harvest Interval							
**or cauliflower, cabbage, Brussel Sprouts, kale							
***summer and winter squashes							
#or peppers and eggplant							

Bordeaux Mix is good against:

- Fire Blight
- Potato Blight
- Black Spot[1]

---

1. http://www.bigblogofgardening.com/organic-garden-photos/summer-vegetable-and-flower-garden-images-2010/

- Peach Leaf Curl
- Downy Mildew
- Powdery Mildew
- Anthracnose
- Late Blight
- Rust

Elemental Sulfur powder – scatter underneath the plants and on lower leaves. The sulfur fumes kill the fungi. Must use gloves, face mask and goggles. Elemental sulfur will burn your eyes.

Dissolved sulfur (0.4%) can be used as a spray for fungal diseases.

Aphids and Ants

There 4,400 species are known, all included in the family *Aphididae*. Approximately, 250 aphid species are serious pests for agriculture[1] and forestry[2]. Aphids vary in length from 1 to 10 millimeters.

There are various kinds of Aphids. Aphids are sucking insects. They suck the sap of plants and secrete a substance called honeydew. This sticky resin is high in sugars and a favorite food of ants and fungi. Often one finds the leaves of the vegetables cover with black mildew where aphids feed. Ants "milk" the aphids by stroking their abdomen. The relationship between aphids and ants is symbiotic. The ants protect the aphids and the aphids provide food for the ants.

Recent scientific studies have found that aphids protect ants from predators, such as lacewings and ladybugs. Ants also protect the aphids from a fungal infection that are lethal, by removing the bodies of the infected aphids.

If you see a large number of ants on a tree or plant, there is a high probably of a large infestation of aphids. Many ant species farm ants.

Aphid's honeydew provides food for ants and they allow themselves to be relocated if the ants require it.

Controlling ants is one way of regulating the aphid population. Ant bait traps are an effective means of control, since ants take the bait back to the colony. The bait kills

---

1. https://en.wikipedia.org/wiki/Agriculture

2. https://en.wikipedia.org/wiki/Forestry

more ants in the colony. A smaller ant population opens the aphids to predators.

Sticky tape can be wrapped around trees to catch the ants. Aphids can be washed off the leaves with organic soapy water sprays or neem oil.

Organic Insecticides

Bacillus Thuringiensis referred to as Bt, is a biological pesticide kills a large variety of worms, moths and beetles.

Beauveria Bassiana is a fungus that infects aphids, caterpillars, grasshoppers, ants and other insects. It replicates until it kills its host. Therefore, concentration is important. It is not an immediate answer to insect infestations.

Kaolin Clay is a type of clay. It can be sprayed as a liquid on annuals. It protects mites, insects, fungi, and harmful bacteria. Kaolin Clay can be used as a powder on trees and bushes. It forms a protective layer between the plants and the pests.

Neem Oil is a brown oil with an unpleasant taste and smell. It acts as a repellent for insects and is non-toxic to humans or honey bees.

Pyrethrum is a natural botanical pesticide. It is made from the dried flowers, *Chrysanthemum cinerariifolium* and *Chrysanthemum coccineum*.

Plant Oils from citrus, canola, mustard, castor and soybean have been used to kill or repel insects.

Preparation of Seedlings

Germination

There are two simple ways of obtaining plants. The first is to buy seedlings or germinate seeds. Most seeds need moisture and heat to germinate. International agreements require that seed have a minimum germination rate of 80%. If your freshly bought seed is not germinating at a minimum of 80%, then return the seed to your supplier. Seed bought in small packets from your local nursery aren't maintained under optimal conditions and they lose their viability quickly. Store seed in a cool dry place.

There is a huge amount of misinformed people writing about seed on the internet. Today four main types of seed are available, landraces, open-pollinated, heirloom, and hybrids.

Landraces are a mixture of similar varieties that grow in a particular area. Pollination is random, and therefore the seed is less uniform, but has a greater genetic diversity, which normally provides a certain about of resistance to diseases within the population.

Open-pollinated (OP) doesn't mean the seed was produce with no controls. That is a landrace. Open-pollinated seed are varieties that are carefully reproduced to that only pollen of the same variety is used. Open pollinated varieties are produced in isolated areas or in protected culture. Open pollinated varieties should give you 98% the exact same variety. Since they are self- pollinated within the population, you get the exact same plant each time you use such seed. Having only one parent, its disease resistance is normally less than that of a hybrid.

Heirloom vegetables are varieties that were used 50-100 years ago. Many are maintained for their unique shapes, color and quality. They should be open-pollinated and therefore each seed should provide you with the same plant each time.

Hybrids are created by crossing two different varieties. To be able to reproduce your results you need two pure-breds (open-pollinated varieties). Hybrids have better vigor, more resistances to insects and diseases, and higher yields. Today in many parts of the world if you don't have hybrids resistant to certain diseases then your crop will be destroyed.

Your greenhouse greatly helps to reduce insect infestations, only if you use it properly. Entering and leaving the greenhouse is the time insects can enter. That is why we designed the MPG with double door systems with positive pressure. When the outside door is opened it turns on the fan creating a barrier against insects coming in. Don't leave the door open unnecessarily. Brush off your clothes before entering. Often insects are on our clothes without our knowledge.

Indicator Plants

Indicator plants are plants that help the farmer determine insect or viral infestation before it becomes an economic disaster.

Thrips carry TSWV (Tomato wilt spot virus and INSV (Impatiens Necrotic Spot Virus). Thrips prefer Petunias and fava bean to other plants if available. Therefore, farmers plant throughout their greenhouse 5-10 plants of Petunias and fava beans. Since the thrips feed on the petunias and fava beans first then regular inspection of these plants will allow the farmer to catch the infestation before it does damage to his crop.

Tagetes (marigold) is another such plant. While it can control root-knot nematodes red spider mite prefer *Tagetes* over all other plants. You will see the webs of the red spider mite on the *Tagetes* several days before it attacks your crop. Rosemary oil is reported to be an alternative spray to kill red spider mites.

Light

Blue Light

The most important blue wavelengths are from 430 to 450 nm. This part of the spectrum is also known as cool light. These wavelengths encourage vegetative growth through strong root growth and intense photosynthesis. Blue light is often used alone during the early phases of plant growth, such as starting seedlings, when flowering is not desired.

Red Light

The longer wavelengths of light are red in color. The most important wavelengths in the red spectrum are from 640 to 680 nm. These wavelengths encourage stem growth, flowering and fruit production, and chlorophyll production. The red wavelengths are known as warm light and they are naturally more prevalent in sunlight during the shorter days of fall and winter.

Green and Yellow Light

Some of the green and yellow light that reaches the plant is reflected, giving the plant a green color. While most of the absorbed wavelengths are in the red and blue ranges, recent research shows that plants do absorb some green and yellow light and use it in the photosynthesis process. A light source that provides light in the entire visible range will better meet the needs of the plant.

Light Intensity

Sunlight provides far greater intensity than artificial lighting. Not all plants need the same light intensities. Some plants prefer the high intensity of full sun, while others prefer moderate sun or shade. In artificial lighting, the plant needs to be close to the light for highest light intensity.

Germination

The vast majority of vegetables and herbs are propagated by seed. Knowing the conditions of maximizing germination will help you produce healthy strong seedlings. Commercial vegetable seed must have at least 85% germination. The percentage of germination is not the only factor. Speed of germination and uniformity of germination are also important. You will find that most seeds that germinate after the majority are spindly and grow into weak plants. If you are using hybrid seed, they are required by international law to be 98% uniform. If your hybrid seed has more than two percent offtypes, then demand new seed.

Germination of seed is enhanced it the seed is primed. The easiest way to prime seed is to soak it in water for 24 hours before planting.

The following tables provide germination information. Table 2 providing the germination temperatures and duration for vegetables and Table 3 for herbs that are compatible to be grown in the greenhouse.

Table 2 Germination Temperatures and Rates

Crop	Germination Temperature °C	Days to germination
Asparagus	21-29	14-56
Bean, Lima	15.5-29.4	6
Bean, Snap	15.5-35	7
Beets	5- 35	4
Broccoli	24-30	4
Brussel Sprouts	20-26.6	4
Cabbage	6-26.6	4
Cauliflower	6-26.6	5
Celeriac	17-21	11
Celery	6-21	7
Cucumber	15.5-35	3
Eggplant	15.5-26.6	6
Kale	15.5-26.6	4
Kohlrabi	15.5-26.6	4
Leek	17-21	7
Lettuce	3-26.6	3
Melon	15.5-29.4	4
Okra	15.5-35	6
Onion	5-26.6	6
Pak Choi	12-26	7
Parsley	7-29.4	13
Parsnip	4-17	14
Pea	15.5-29.4	6
Pepper	15.5-29.4	8
Pumpkin	15.5-35	4
Radish	7-29.9	4
Rutabaga	21-27	4

Spinach	5-22	5
Squash	15.5-36	4
Swiss Chard	7-27	4
Tomato	12-29	6
Turnip	8-29	3
Watermelon	16-36	4

Fertilizer Requirements

Table 3 outlines the general total nitrogen needs of vegetables and herbs during their growing season.

Table 3. General Nitrogen Needs of Greenhouse Crops

Age of Plant	Total Nitrogen in ppm
0-4 weeks	20-30
4-6 weeks	30-50
6-8 weeks	50-65
8-11 weeks	65-75
11-15 weeks	70-85

Another general rule of preparing fertilizer. Mix one bag of 25 kg of fertilizer with 100 liters of water to be your stock solution. Full grown plant needs 2% of this stock solution injected into the water system.

Irrigation Requirements

There have not been a lot of studies conducted on the water usage of plants. A rule of thumb is to have available 12 to 16.5 liters/square meter of growing area per day as a peak use rate for the hottest day. For example, a 6-meter x 4-meter net growing area is 24 sq. meters. At peak requirement you need to irrigate at a rate of 288 to 396 liters per day. This corresponds with the evapotranspiration rate for most areas of the country. The following factors can increase or decrease the amount of water needed:

Radiation-high radiation causes an increase in water needs.

Shade- reduces transpiration and reduces water needs.

Air movement- Increases transpiration and increases water needs.

Plant Size- As the plant grows it needs more water.

Leaching- this is adding extra water to wash out excess salts in your growing media.

Type of Irrigation-the efficiency of the irrigation system will alter the amount of water you use.

Water quality-Water with high electric conductivity (EC measures the amount of salts in the water) will require leaching the soil.

If you have a scale there is a simple method to determine water needs. Thoroughly water the plants in the morning and let them drain for at least 30 minutes. Then weigh the pots, come back 24 hours later and weigh the pots again. The decrease in weight is the amount of water that has been used by the plant. Water use will differ from day to day.

Even in artificial media systems, irrigation signifies a large and potentially important loss of nutrients. Irrigation is also a source of environmental pollution as a surplus of 20% to 50% of the plant's water uptake in each irrigation cycle is often recommended. Indeed, annual use of irrigation water ranges from 150 to 200 mm (e.g., leafy vegetable) in soil-based greenhouse crops to 1000 to 1500 mm in soilless-grown (e.g., Solanaceae, cucurbits). For container nursery production, as cited by Fulcher et al., those values could be as high as 2900 mm.

Tensiometers

A tensiometer measures soil moisture. It is designed to measure the tension that plants' roots must apply to remove water from the soil. The tension measured by the tensiometer is a direct measure of the availability of water to a plant. Tensiometers can be employed in any irrigated crop either outdoors or under protected culture. They provide data to aid the grower in his irrigation decisions. With crops that have high water requirements or where any wilting will damage yields, tensiometers are a good aid to irrigation needs.

Tensiometers must be inserted into the soil at the midpoint of the main fibrous root system. There irrigation water is sure to wet the soil and at the bottom of the root zone.

Correct placement is crucial. Placed too deep in a shallow rooted crop and the readings will cause you to irrigate too late, thus causing water stress. Improper placement in a deep-rooted crop, will result in unnecessary irrigation and water logging. To avoid excessive irrigation, place the tensiometer at the bottom of the root zone to check subsoil moisture and drainage.

Growing Vegetables

Beans:

Beans are of the easiest vegetables to grow. The seeds are planted directly in the growth medium, germinate quickly and grow vigorously. This vegetable is a warm season crop and supply a good harvest in a small space. There are a very large variety of beans divided into two groups either bush or pole beans.

Growing media: Any artificial media

Soil pH. 6.0-6.5

Seed Spacing – Bush types: 8 cm apart and 2 cm deep;

Pole types: Plant two rows 15 cm apart. Two seeds every 8cm in

the row. Place the pole of string down the middle of the two rows. Thin later to one seed on each side of the trellis string.

Germination temperatures: 21 – 32°C

Maturity - Bush: 50-60 days; Pole 60-70 days

Planting times– In our greenhouse if properly heated and cooled all year long. If you want all year around production, plant every two weeks.

Planting instructions – Soak the seed in water for 24 hours before planting for both bush and pole varieties in rows. Half an hour before planting add Baking Soda to the water. High pH kills fungi. The seed coat of the seeds will wrinkle and the seed size will increase significantly after soaking in water. This pretreatment will cause a more rapid and uniform germination of your seed.

Companion Planting

Positive affect: beet, cabbage, carrot, corn, squash, tomato

Negative affect: chive, fennel, garlic, leek

Watering & Fertilizer:

Bean leaves are susceptible to various diseases if their leaves are constantly wet. I recommend drip irrigation. If you have an irrigation computer, give the beans at least two waterings a day to avoid water stress. Don't over water.

5-10-10, which is good for beans, indicates the fertilizer contains 5% nitrogen, 10% phosphorus and 10% potassium

Weeding- weed by hand or use the recommended organic herbicide listed above.

Disease & Insects - These plants need good air circulation. Do not harvest or work around them when plants are wet, this may spread disease. The major diseases that affect beans are:

White mold[1] Bean common mosaic virus[2]

Rust[3] Bronzing and sunscald[4]

Bacterial blight[5] Anthracnose[6]

Root rots[7] Angular leaf spot[8]

Damping off[9] Alternaria leaf spot[10]

see section on organic fungal control above.

Common Insect Infestations:

Aphis

Leafhoppers

1. http://www.extension.umn.edu/garden/yard-garden/vegetables/edible-bean-disease-and-disorder-identification/#white-mold

2. http://www.extension.umn.edu/garden/yard-garden/vegetables/edible-bean-disease-and-disorder-identification/#mosaic-virus

3. http://www.extension.umn.edu/garden/yard-garden/vegetables/edible-bean-disease-and-disorder-identification/#rust

4. http://www.extension.umn.edu/garden/yard-garden/vegetables/edible-bean-disease-and-disorder-identification/#bronzing-and-sunscald

5. http://www.extension.umn.edu/garden/yard-garden/vegetables/edible-bean-disease-and-disorder-identification/#bacterial-blight

6. http://www.extension.umn.edu/garden/yard-garden/vegetables/edible-bean-disease-and-disorder-identification/#anthracnose

7. http://www.extension.umn.edu/garden/yard-garden/vegetables/edible-bean-disease-and-disorder-identification/#root-rots

8. http://www.extension.umn.edu/garden/yard-garden/vegetables/edible-bean-disease-and-disorder-identification/#angular-leaf-spot

9. http://www.extension.umn.edu/garden/yard-garden/vegetables/edible-bean-disease-and-disorder-identification/#damping-off

10. http://www.extension.umn.edu/garden/yard-garden/vegetables/edible-bean-disease-and-disorder-identification/#alternaria-leaf-spot

Mexican Bean Beetle

Seed Corn Maggots

Red Spider Mite

see section of organic insect control above.

Harvest- Pick your string or snap varieties every few days by pulling the pod with one hand while holding the plant with the other. Do not harvest if plants are wet as they will not store well. Smaller vegetables taste tenderer. Dried varieties need to be harvested when the plant has matured fully. Dry beans should be allowed to stay on the plant until leaves fall off and pods are dry.

Storage- Fresh beans can be stored in the refrigerator for two weeks in a plastic bag. Only wash them when you are ready to use them

Nutritionally, beans provide good amounts of carbohydrates, potassium, dietary fiber, B-6, magnesium and minor amounts of other vitamins and micro-elements.

Beets

Beets have a long harvest, long storage life and produce a lot in a small space. The young leaves (7-10 cm) can be used fresh for salads. The bulb can be used from the size of 6 cm in diameter.

Soil pH: 6.2 to 7.0

Growing media: Any media that will not restrict the expansion of the bulb. Planting your beets:

Seed Spacing – 4 cm apart 2 cm deep; Once the plants have germinated thin them to 8 cm apart to allow space for the bulbs to develop.

When using transplants space 8 cm apart.

Germinate in growth media at temperatures of 15 to 26 °C.

Days to Maturity - 50-60 days

Planting times–You can plant in your Mini Professional Greenhouse at any time of the year that you are growing other crops that you are growing warm weather crops.

Companion Planting

Positive effect: cabbage

Negative effect: runner bean or any plant which will cause shading.

Watering – Irrigate twice a day to keep the growth

media moist. Don't over water.

Fertilizer: 10N-10P-10K

Weeding - Keep weeded while plants are small.

Diseases

Cercospora leaf spot.

Damping-off.

Bacterial blight.

Downy mildew.

Powdery mildew.

Black root rot.

Insects - Leaf miner, beet web worm, root-knot nematode.

Harvest - Leaf: cut individual leaves when 8-10 cm for salad. These must be cooled quickly by putting them in cold water. Root: harvest by pulling the whole plant when they are the size of a golf ball or larger.

Storage- When storing cut off the beet greens leaving at least an inch of stem and then store the greens and roots separately. Place the greens in a plastic bag and use within a few days. Store the roots in the refrigerator for up to 3 weeks. If you have a large amount store in a box packed with peat or straw.

Nutritionally, beets provide small amounts of vitamins, iron, electrolytes, and micro-elements.

Broccoli

Broccoli prefers cool weather to grow. Plant in the early spring for summer or early fall harvest and early summer for late fall harvesting. Small heads called side shoots will form on the stem after the large head is harvested. These can be cut and used to extend your harvest. These vegetables are best transplanted as they get more growth before the heat of summer.

Botanical Family -Brassicaeae/Mustard Family

Soil pH 6.0-6.8.

Broccoli planting info:

Seed spacing–30-35 cm apart. Germinate in growth media temperature of 15 to 30°C.

Days to Maturity - 50-72 days

Planting times–If you have set your greenhouse to the environmental conditions for Brassica, then you and grow this crop all year long. Best to sow broccoli in seedlings trays and then transplant at 5-7 weeks

Planting Instruction- Seeds need to be covered when seeded in propagating mix (use large cells). Add a handful of compost in the hole when transplanting. Water it well.

Companion Planting

Positive effects: bean, dill, onion, potato, oregano, sage

Negative effects: tomato, lettuce

Watering - Water regularly once a day at the base of the plants with drip irrigation. If the temperature goes over 28°C, water twice a day.

Fertilizer: 10N-10P-10K according to instructions above.

Weeding - Keep weeded while plants are small.

Diseases

Club root–soil fungus

Powdery mildew

Downy mildew

Botrytis

Insects-

Root maggot

Cabbage worm

Cabbage Loopers

Army Worms

Cabbage root fly

Aphids

Harvest- Pick the center head when it is at least 5 inches across. After the center head is cut many smaller side shoots will develop.

Storage- Cool as soon as you harvest buy putting it on ice or in the fridge. This vegetable will keep in the refrigerator of up to 2 weeks.

Nutritionally, broccoli provides large amounts of vitamin C. Broccoli is a good source of dietary fiber, pantothenic acid, vitamin B6, vitamin E, manganese, phosphorus, choline, vitamin B1, vitamin A (in the form of carotenoids), potassium and copper. This vegetable also is a good source of vitamin B1, magnesium, omega-3 fatty acids, protein, zinc, calcium, iron, niacin and selenium.

Brussel Sprouts

Brussel sprouts prefer cool weather to grow. Plant in the early spring for late fall harvesting. Small heads will develop on the stem. These vegetables are best transplanted as they get more growth before the heat of summer.

Botanical Family- Brassicaeae/Mustard Family

Soil pH 6.0-6.8.

Seed spacing - 40 cm apart

Germinate in soil temperature of 10 – 30 C

Days to Maturity - 45 days to several months

Planting times- Sow April to mid-July; transplants at 6-8 weeks.

Planting Instruction- Seeds need to be covered when seeded in propagating mix (use large cells). Add a handful of compost in the hole when transplanting. Water it well a firm down.

Companion Planting

Positive effects: bean, beet, dill nasturtium, onion, potato, oregano

Negative effects: tomato, strawberry, lettuce

Watering- Water regularly once a day at the base of the plants with drip irrigation. If the temperature goes over 28°C, water twice a day.

Fertilizer: 10N-10P-10K according to instructions above.

Weeding – by hand or salt-vinegar mix spray.

Diseases

Club root – soil fungus

Powdery mildew

Downy mildew

Botrytis

Insects -

Root maggot

Cabbage worm –

Cabbage Loopers

Army Worms

Cabbage root fly

Aphids

Harvest When picking remove the leaf beneath the sprout and then cut or break off the sprout. Sprouts that are 1 - 1 1/2 inches in diameter are the best tasting.

Storage Will keep fresh for up to a week in the refrigerator. They can be frozen for future use.

Nutritionally, once cup of Brussel sprouts contains just 56 calories. It has more than 240 percent of the recommended daily amount for vitamin K1, and nearly 130 percent of vitamin C. Plus, Brussels sprouts can be a good source of fiber, manganese, potassium, choline, and B vitamins.

Cabbage

Cabbage prefers cool weather to grow. Plant in the early spring for summer or early fall harvest and early summer for late fall harvesting. Small heads will develop on the stem after the large head is harvested. These can be cut and used to extend your harvest. These vegetables are best transplanted as they get more growth before the heat of summer.

Botanical Family - Brassicaeae/Mustard Family

Soil pH: 6.0-6.5

Soil Preparation- Grows well after a green manure crop. Dig in a few inches of compost or aged manure, shredded leaves and lime (5 pounds per 50-foot bed) before planting. Use compost or manure tea at bud formation time. These vegetable plants benefit by a sprinkling of salt water before they form heads. The salt water hinders the growth of caterpillars.

Planting your cabbage:

Seed Info-

Seed spacing - 18 inches apart

Germinate in soil temperature

of 10 – 30 C

Days to Maturity - 45 days to

several months

Planting times - Sow April to mid-July; transplants at 6-8 weeks. Set out before they reach 6-8 leaf stage. Succession plants every 2 weeks.

Planting Instruction - Seeds need to be covered when seeded in propagating mix (use large cells). Add a handful of compost in the hole when transplanting. After planting water well.

Companion Planting

Positive affect: bean, beet, dill,

Nasturtium, onion, potato, oregano.

Negative affect: tomato, strawberry

Watering- Water regularly once a day at the base of the plants with drip irrigation. If the temperature goes over 28°C, water twice a day.

Fertilizer: 10N-10P-10K according to instructions above.

Weeding - Keep weeded while plants are small.

Diseases

Club root – soil fungus

Powdery mildew

Downy mildew

Botrytis

Insects-

Root maggot

Cabbage worm –

Cabbage Loopers

Army Worms

Cabbage root fly

Aphids

Harvest - Heads are ready when they are firm to the touch. Heads may split after reaching maturity. Pick before a hard frost.

Storage - Cut individual heads and keep in your refrigerator up to 2 weeks, if you have a large amount pull up the plant roots included. Wrap in newspaper and place in a box and keep at 0 degree. Can be frozen for future use.

Nutritionally, cabbage provides 60% of the recommended daily vitamin C. Cabbage has small amounts of various vitamin Bs and minor amounts of other micro-elements.

Cauliflower

Cauliflower prefers cool weather to grow. Plant in the early spring for summer or early fall harvest and early summer for late fall harvesting. These vegetables are best transplanted as they get more growth before the heat of summer.

Botanical Family - Brassicaeae/Mustard Family

Soil pH (6.0-6.8.

Soil Preparation - Grows well after a green manure crop. Dig in a few inches of compost or aged manure, shredded leaves and lime (5lbs per 50' bed) before planting. Use compost or manure tea at bud formation time.

Seed Info-

Seed spacing - 18 inches apart

Germinate in soil temperature of 10 – 30 C

Days to Maturity - 45 days to several months

Planting times - Sow April to mid-July; transplants at 6-8 weeks. Set out before they reach 6-8 leaf stage. Succession plants every 2 weeks.

Planting Instruction - Seeds need to be covered when seeded in propagating mix (use large cells). Add a handful of compost in the hole when transplanting. Water it well a firm down.

Companion Planting

Positive effects: bean, beet, dill nasturtium, onion, potato, oregano

Negative effects: tomato, strawberry, lettuce

Watering- Water regularly once a day at the base of the plants with drip irrigation. If the temperature goes over 28°C, water twice a day.

Fertilizer: 10N-10P-10K according to instructions above.

Weeding- Keep weeded while plants are small.

Diseases

Club root – soil fungus

Powdery mildew

Downy mildew

Botrytis

Insects -

Root maggot

Cabbage worm –

Cabbage Loopers

Army Worms

Cabbage root fly

Aphids

Harvest - Pick the head when it is 5-8 inches and before the segments begin to separate.

Storage - Cool as soon as you harvest. This vegetable will keep in the refrigerator for several weeks.

Nutritionally, cauliflower provides a good amount of vitamin C and only minor amounts of the other vitamins and micro-elements

Celery

Celery needs a long cool growing season; it needs even constant weather without cold or dry periods. This vegetable can be difficult to grow in the home garden, but do not give up hope. It needs more attention than most vegetables but can be very rewarding when it grows well. I always start my seeds indoors about 8-10 weeks before I am ready to plant them out into the garden. Learn more about propagating here. In the grocery store the stalks are whitish in color, so you will have to blanch them if this is what you want. For blanching, the stalks need to be covered with paper or cloth for at least a month. I do not mind eating green stalks they taste just as good.

Botanical Family – *Apium graveolens*

Celery is a long-season crop that can be difficult to grow. It likes fertile soil, cool temperatures, and constant moisture. It will not tolerate heat and can be hard to transplant.

Soil –Any growth media; pH 6.0-7.0

Seed Info -

Seed Spacing - Space between plants is 8 inches

in rows 12 inches apart.

Germinate in warm soil temperature;

transplanting is best

Days to Maturity - 90-135 days

Planting Times - Plant in late spring.

Companion Planting

Positive affect: Beans, brassicas, spinach, squash,

tomato, cucumber

Negative affect: Carrot, parsnips

Blanching is the act of covering plant parts to prevent photosynthesis, making the covered parts a pale yellowish green. Blanching celery stalks is to prevent them from becoming bitter. Self-blanching varieties are available. To blanch celery, cover the bottom of the stalks with growth media. This can be done slowly throughout the season or during the last two weeks before harvesting. Alternatively, newspaper or cardboard can be tied around the stalks or boards can be erected around the plants to block out sunlight

Watering Twice a day at the base of the plants with drip irrigation. If the temperature goes over 28°C, water three times a day.

Fertilizer: 10N-10P-10K according to instructions above.

Weeding– Control weeds by hand or the recommended organic herbicide mentioned above.

Pests:

Aphids (Carrot-willow aphids, Peach aphid, Hawthorn aphid,

Melon aphid).

Army worms

Root-knot nematode

Diseases

Bacterial blight

Celery Mosaic Virus (CeMV)

Pithium

Rhizoctonia

Downy mildew

Cercospora leaf spot

Fusarium

Septoria leaf blight)

Sclerotinia

Harvest- Cut the stalks off at the base individually or as a whole plant.

Storage - Stalks can be stored up to 2 weeks in the refrigerator if kept in a plastic bag.

Nutritionally, 100 gm of celery provides less than 10% of the daily needs of vitamins and micro-elements.

Cucumbers

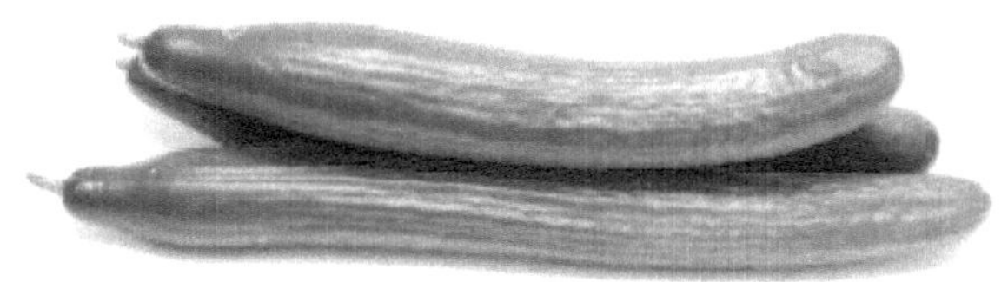

Growing cucumbers is not complicated. There are many hybrids of various types available. For greenhouse production the best is parthenocarpic hybrids. Parthenocarpic plants set fruit at each flower without the need of pollination. They have soft rudimentary seeds inside the fruit that are easy to eat. Most of these hybrids have edible skins. Greenhouse cucumbers need to be trellised. Hang strings from the support cables.

Cucumbers contain three lignans lariciresinol, pinoresinol, and secoisolariciresinol—that have been shown to reduce risk of cardiovascular disease as well as several cancer types, including breast, uterine, ovarian, and prostate cancers. One hundred grams of cucumbers have 19% of your daily need for vitamin K and 12% of the molybdenum.

Botanical Family – *Cucurbitaceae*, Melons,

squashes, cucumbers

Soil – any growth media.

Media Preparation – Give a pre-planting irrigation. Don't transplant into dry media.

Seed Info -

Seed Spacing – 1 seed per cell in your seedling

tray

Best seed germination is at 30 C.

Days to Maturity - 50-65 days

Planting times - Soak seeds in water for 24 hours before planting in 1x1 inch hole sized seedling trays. Cucumbers can be planted all year long in the mini professional greenhouse.

Planting Instruction – Allow the seedlings to grow in their trays for four weeks. Make sure there is good contact between the roots of the seedling and its new growth media. Water after transplanting.

Companion Planting

Positive affect: bean, broccoli, cabbage, lettuce,

pea, radish, tomato

Negative affect: sage

Watering- Water regularly once a day at the base of the plants with drip irrigation. If the temperature goes over 28°C, water twice a day.

Fertilizer. 10N-10P-10K according to instructions above.

Trellising – The vast majority of greenhouse cucumbers are parthenocarpic (don't need pollination to set fruit) and indeterminate (keeps growing upward). Hang a support steel cable or thick nylon rope (8mm) across the rows of cucumbers. Then tie a large loop of thin nylon string around the support cable. Let the string fall until it reaches the ground. Then tie the bottom of the string to your growing vessel. One to two times a week, twist the growing vine around the support string.

Weeding–Weed by hand or use the recommended organic herbicide listed above.

Insects –

Spotted Cucumber Beetle

Red Spider Mite

Melon Aphids

Squash Bugs

Squash Vine Borer

Pickle Worms

Squash Beetle

Diseases

Anthracnose

Downy mildew

Powdery mildew

Gummy stem blight

Alternaria leaf spot

Scab

Cercospora leaf spot

Harvest - When plants are 6-12 inches long cut the fruit with a knife. It you twist it off you may break the stalk which may kill the plant. Harvest in the morning when it is cool. Picking when young will encourage more fruit.

Storage - Best stored in the refrigerator wrapped in plastic. Fresh picked will keep up to a week. Cucumbers should be stored in the refrigerator where they will keep for several days. Cucumbers should not be left out at room temperature for too long as this will cause them to wilt and become limp.

Nutritionally, cucumbers provide minor amounts of vitamins and micro-elements.

Eggplant

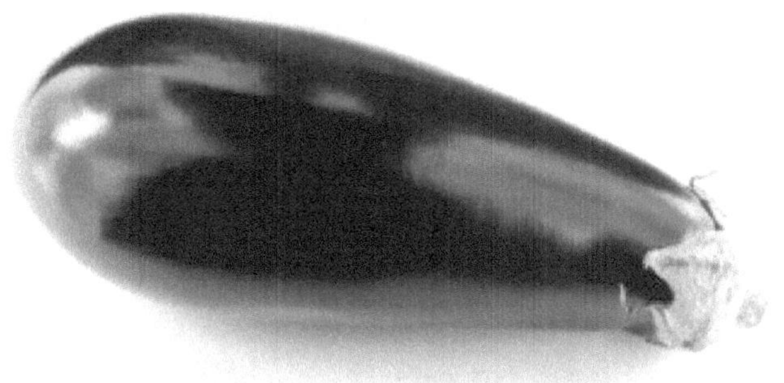

Eggplant is in the same family as tomatoes or peppers and need the same kind of care. There are purple and white varieties. They need lots of heat and rich soil to grow their best. I get best results starting them indoors at the same time as my tomato plants. This is not a common plant home gardeners grow, however if you enjoy eating and cooking with this vegetable it is a wonderful addition to the garden.

Botanical Family – *Solanaceae,* Nightshade

family

Soil - Good, rich, slightly on the acidic side.

Eggplant needs a lot of nutrients[1] to grow well.

Seed Info

Seed Spacing - 12 inches apart

Germinate in soil temperature of 24 - 32 C

Days to Maturity - 70-80 days

Planting times - Sow indoor April 1-15; transplant

---

1. http://your-vegetable-gardening-helper.com/soil-fertilizers.html

mid to late June.

Planting Instruction - Add handful of compost[2] to hole when transplanting. Needs lots of warmth; use clear plastic cloche or greenhouse. Cool temperatures will encourage leafy growth but no fruit.

Companion Planting

pea, thyme, tarragon

Watering- - Require lots of water to avoid it from being bitter. Water regularly once a day at the base of the plants with drip irrigation. If the temperature goes over 28°C, water twice a day.

Fertilizer: 10N-10P-10K according to instructions above.

Weeding - Keep weeded when plants are small.

Insects –

Flea beetles

Lace bug

Aphids

Colorado potato beetle

Red spider.

Diseases

Bacterial Wilt

Cercospora Leaf Spot

---

2. http://your-vegetable-gardening-helper.com/compost.html

Damping off (Pythium)

Alternaria rot

Anthracnose

Fusarium Wilt

Verticillium Wilt

Southern Blight

Eggplant Mosaic Virus (EMV)

Harvest - Eggplant can have a taste bitter if picked when under ripe or overripe. Harvesting eggplant is an art. A flawless fruit will stop growing larger, have a glossy skin, and will have soft, well-formed yet immature seeds. Fruits with dark seeds are overripe eggplants. Don't pull or twist the fruit off the plant. Cut the eggplant off with a knife leaving a 2cm of stem,

Storage- Store in a plastic bag in the warmer section of the refrigerator to protect against excess cold temperatures that can cause the development of pitted mushy spots. They will keep up to 5 days this way.

Nutritionally eggplants provide have very little value.

Garlic

The portion of the garlic plant we eat is in actuality its seeds.

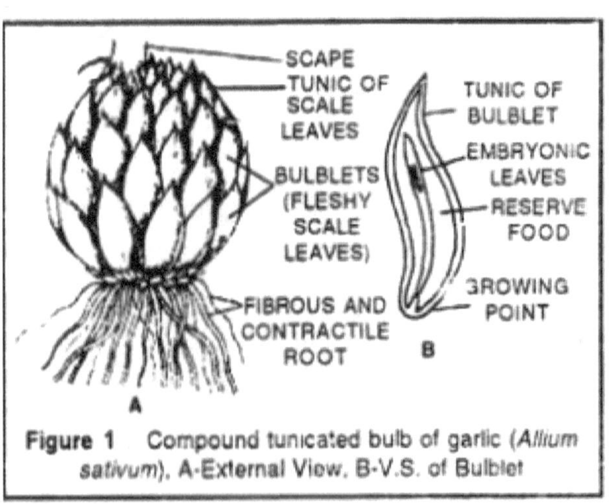

Figure 1   Compound tunicated bulb of garlic (*Allium sativum*), A-External View, B-V.S. of Bulblet

Garlic produces a group of cloves encased in a sheath. The best cloves for replanting are the large outside ones. Garlic has been used for thousands of years for both cooking and medicine. Dr. Norman Walker recommended juiced garlic for dissolving accumulated mucus, helps exudate poisons through the pores of the skin, promotes peristalsis and diuretic action, good against dysentery and all kinds of parasites (Norman, 1936)

Botanical Name: *Allium sativum*

Soil pH 6.0-6.8,

Seed Info

Seed Spacing - 3 rows/30-inch bed; 12 inches

apart; 2 inches deep

Days to Maturity – 5-6 months usually ready in

late June the following year.

Planting times - Sow direct on October 1st through to January

Planting Instruction - Plant clove pointed end up. Upside down cloves rarely germinate. Do not remove the skin from the clove. Plant 9-11 cm apart and 4-5 cm deep.

Companion Planting

Positive affect: carrot, tomato

Negative affect: bean, pea, strawberry

Watering–keep moist, but not wet, to avoid rotting. Water regularly once a day at the base of the plants with drip irrigation. If the temperature goes over 28°C, water twice a day.

Fertilizer: 10N-10P-10K according to instructions above.

Weeding– by hand or by the recommended herbicide from above.

Disease

Basal Rot (*Fusarium culmorum*),

White Rot (*Sclerotium cepivorum*),

Downy Mildew (*Peronospora destructor*),

Botrytis Rot *(Botrytis porri)*

Penicillium Decay (*Penicillium hirsutum*).

Mosaic Virus Garlic mosaic virus (GarMV) ...

Purple blotch Fungi (*Alternaria porri)*

Rust Fungus (*Puccinia porri*)

Insects–

Bulb mites (*Arachnid Rhizoglyphus spp.*)

Leafminers Insects (*Lyriomyza* spp.)

Lesion nematode Nematode (*Pratylenchus penetrans*).

Onion maggot Insect (*Delia antiqua*).

Harvest - Pull the whole plant when tops begin to die back. Let plants dry in the sun for 3-4 days. Cut off the tops to about 3 cm or braid them. Clean them up a bit by cutting off most of the root from the bottom of the bulb.

Storage - Store in paper bags or boxes or hanging in the air by their braids. Do not wash before storing.

Nutritionally, garlic has good amounts of potassium, vitamin C and B-6. It also has iron, calcium, magnesium and dietary fiber.

Kale

Kale is a cool season crop that will overwinter well. Flavor improves after a frost. If provided with shade you can be planted in early spring to be harvested in the summer. Kale matures quickly, is full of nutrients and can be eaten raw or cooked. It can be harvested as a whole plant or by cutting off lower leaves as you need them.

Botanical Family -Brassicaeae/Mustard Family

Soil pH (6.5-6.8).

Seed Info-

Seed Spacing – 35-40 cm apart

Germinate in soil temperature of 10 - 30C

Days to Maturity - 50-72 days

Planting Instruction– Grow kale with other Brassica species which like cool temperatures. You can direct seed or started as transplants. If direct seeding, plant every 20 cm and then thin them out once they are 10-12 cm tall.

Companion Planting

Positive effect: bean, dill, nasturtium, onion, potato, oregano, sage

Negative effect: lettuce, tomato

Watering- Water regularly once a day at the base of the plants with drip irrigation. If the temperature goes over 28°C, water twice a day.

Fertilizer. 10N-10P-10K according to instructions above.

Weeding- by hand or by the recommended herbicide from above.

Disease

 Alternaria leaf spot (Black spot, Gray spot)

 Fungus *Alternaria brassicae.*

 Black rot (Leaf spot) Bacteria *Xanthomonas campestris.*

Insects -.

 Cabbage aphid Insect *Brevicoryne brassicaea.*

 Cabbage looper Insect *Trichoplusia ni.*

 Cutworms Insects *Agrotis spp*.

.[1] Beet armyworm Insect Spodoptera exigua.

---

1. https://www.plantvillage.org/en/topics/kale/diseases_and_pests_description_uses_propagation

Harvest - Cut outer leaves when they are 15 cm or more in length. Once the plant starts producing smaller leaves cut the whole plant. Must be cooled quickly.

Storage - Is best stored in a sealed plastic bag or container in the refrigerator. It is best to use kale within a few days as it has a short shelf life.

Nutritionally, kale is very rich in vitamin A and C. It also has some iron, calcium, magnesium, lutein, zeaxanthin (excellent for improving your eye sight) and vitamin B-6.

Leeks

Leeks belong to the onion family. They need similar conditions to grow. Leeks prefer cool temperatures, rich soil and lots of water especially early in their growth. This vegetable is grown from seed and then transplanted to your garden. Leeks are slow growing. From seed to seedlings can take 2-3 months before they are e ready to be planted out. Similar to celery flavor can be improved by putting a mound of soil around the stem. Like celery this can be done gradually by adding soil throughout the season.

Botanical Family: Amaryllis: Onion family

Soil pH: 6.0-6.8. Will tolerate moderately acid soil but is must be rich in nitrogen.

Seed Info

Seed Spacing – 12-18 cm apart; 1.5-2 cm deep

Germinate in soil temperature of 10-25 C

Days to Maturity - 75-125 days

Planting Instruction - Use a large stick or narrow shovel to make 15-18 cm deep holes. Place the transplants at the bottom of the hole. Cover the transplant with soil up to the first leaf notch. Leave the rest of the hole unfilled. You can fill the hole gradually to blanch the stem.

Companion Planting

Positive affect: carrot, celery

Negative affect: bean, pea, strawberry

Watering- During early stages leeks require an abundance of water. Adjust the amount of water as it grows. Water regularly once a day at the base of the plants with drip irrigation. If the temperature goes over 28°C, water twice a day.

Fertilizer. 10N-10P-10K according to instructions above.

Weeding- Keep weeded while plants are small.

Disease –

Botrytis leaf blight Fungus *Botrytis squamosa*.

Damping-off Fungi *Fusarium spp.*

Downy mildew Fungi *Peronospora parasitica*.

Pink root Fungus *Phoma terrestris*.

Purple blotch Fungi *Alternaria porri.*

Insects –

Leafminers Insects *Lyriomyza spp*.

Onion maggot Insect *Delia antiqua.*

Thrips Insect *Thrips tabaci*.

Harvest - Leeks can be picked when the stalk is 2.4 cm or larger in diameter.

Storage - Store in an airtight plastic bag in the refrigerator crisper. They should keep for at least a week.

Nutritionally, leeks have vitamin A, C and small amounts of B-6. They also have some magnesium, iron and calcium.

Lettuce and Salad Greens

Lettuce and salad greens grow well in hydroponics. They are fast and easy to grow in garden beds or containers. Lettuce is divided into two types, the head and leaf varieties.

Heading types take longer to mature and therefore need a longer cooler growing season. They also do better in full sun. This variety does best as transplants. They get a good growth before the weather warms up.

The leaf varieties are more popular, grow quicker and will tolerate some shade. If you scatter the seeds of leaf varieties, they do not need thinning as you can start cutting them once they reach about 3 inches. There are many types of salad mixes available which are great as you get a variety of different seeds in one package.

The young leaves of Japanese mustard greens, arugula, mustard, kale, Swiss chard, spinach are all used as salad greens.

Botanical Name: *Lactuca sativa*

Soil pH 6.0-6.8.

Soil Preparation - Seed Info

Seed Spacing - 12 inches apart to grow to maturity

or can be broadcast for early cutting

Germinate in soil temperature of 10 – 27 C

Days to Maturity - Lettuce - 50-75 days; Salad

Greens - 21-30 days

Fertilizer – 10N-10P-10K

Planting Instruction - Provide some shade during the summer months. Thermal blanket will work well.

Companion Planting

Positive affect: beet, cabbage, pea, clover, radish, strawberry

Negative affect: none

> **Watering** - Regular watering; water more often during the hottest part of summer.

Weeding - Keep weeded.

Disease

Big vein Virus Mirafiori lettuce big-vein virus (MiLBVV)

Bottom rot Fungus *Rhizoctonia solani.*

Downy mildew Fungus *Bremia lactucae.*

Leaf drop Fungi *Sclerotinia minor.*

Powdery mildew Fungus *Erysiphe cichoracearum.*

Insects -

Slugs

Aphids.

Armyworms.

Corn earworms.

Crickets.

Darkling beetles.

Flea beetles.

Garden symphylans

Grasshoppers.

Harvest - Harvest early in the morning before sun hits them or spray them with water before picking. Cut the lettuce just above the base with a sharp knife. The plant will grow back. The new leaves can be used as salad greens.

Storage – Lettuce likes high humidity and cool temperatures. Wash leaves, dry them, and then store in a tightly sealed plastic container. It helps to place a cloth at the bottom to soak up moisture. Lettuce can last in the refrigerator for 5-7 days.

Nutritionally, lettuce is rich in Vitamin A. It has small amounts of vitamin C, B-6, iron and magnesium.

Melon

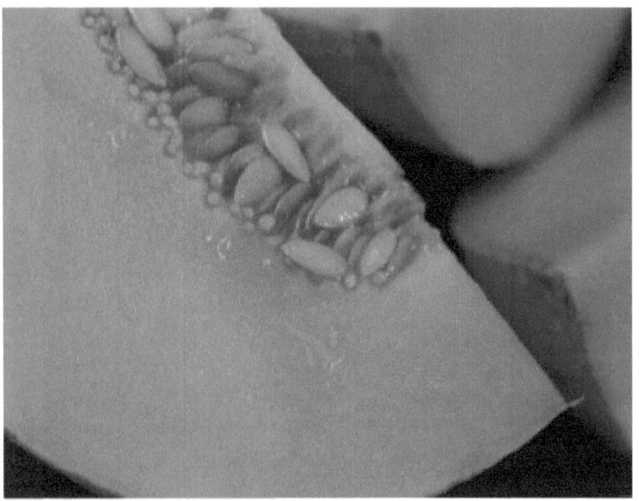

Melon quality—flavor, aroma, texture, and sweetness—is best when the sugar content of the fruit is high. Sweet melons need lots of sunlight, warm temperatures, enough water, and freedom from diseases and insects.

Plant stress, whether from insects, leaf diseases, weeds, poor nutrition, too much or too little water, or cold or cloudy conditions, will prevent the fruits from creating enough sugar.

Botanical Family: *Cucurbitaceae*, Melons,

squashes, cucumbers

Soil pH: 60-6.5

Seeding

Sow your seeds in seedling trays with at least 2.4 x

2.4 cm cells.

Transplant

Transplant seedlings when they are 15-20 cm tall. Plant them every 30 cm.

Choosing a Compatible Variety

To grow melons in a greenhouse, one must chose a variety with smaller fruit. Vines need to be trellised and if the fruit is too large and heavy, it will fall off the vine before it is ripe.

Trim the plant to one main stem which you will trellis.

Watering- Water regularly once a day at the base of the plants with drip irrigation. If the temperature goes over 28°C, water twice a day.

Fertilizer. 10N-10P-10K according to instructions above.

How to Plant Melons

Though one may sow directly into your growing media, it is better to prepare seedlings in trays. Consider installing protective row covers after you finish planting melons. Row covers benefit melons by raising soil surface temperatures, taming wind and excluding insects. Remove covers a week after plants begin to bloom so insects can pollinate the flowers (learn more about how to use row covers[1] to protect plants and extend your growing season).

Insects

Beet armyworm

Cabbage aphid

Cabbage Looper

---

1. http://www.motherearthnews.com/organic-gardening/no-spray-way-to-protect-plants.aspx

Flea Beetle

Mango Fruit Fly

Melon Aphid

Melon Thrips

Red Spider Mite

White Fly

Diseases

Bacterial fruit blotch

Fusarium wilt

Gummy stem blight

Powdery mildew

Sudden wilt

Tomato root-knot nematodes

Papaya ringspot virus-type W

Watermelon mosaic virus-2

Zucchini yellows mosaic virus

Improve Quality

Seven to ten days before harvest turnoff or radically reduce the amount of water you are giving the melon plants. Excess water reduces the flavor which is a combination of flavonoids, sugar and acid. The taste of most fruit is dependent on the sugar: acid ratio. Too little acid and the fruit tastes flat. Too much acid and the fruit tastes sour. Melons naturally have very little acid.

How to Pick a Melon

You know a melon is ripe by its smell. If it has no or little typical 'melon' smell then it is not ripe. The fruit should be firm. If the fruit is soft anywhere then it is either overripe or infected.

Most muskmelons naturally separate ("slip") from the vine when they are ripe. A gentle tug should cause the melon to detach if it is ripe. The rinds of some varieties of honeydew and watermelon change color when ripe, making it easier to learn the melon-picker's art. Many types of melons have netting on the skin. A good high-quality melon will have full netting. Blotchy netting is another sign of lower quality.

Nutritionally, melons provide a great source of vitamin C and vitamin A, in the form of carotenoids. Melons are an excellent source of vitamin A. They also provide potassium, and B vitamins (thiamine, niacin, and folate), vitamin K, magnesium, and fiber in small amounts.

Onions

Onions like a cool temperature to start and then need heat to form a large bulb. This vegetable is grown from sets, seeds or transplants. Onions are categorized by the daylength in which they are grown, long day, medium day and short day. The greenhouse is set up for long days (15.5 hours a day of light).

Sets consist of small dry bulbs that are grown and harvested the previous year for the purpose of being replanted and grown to produce bulbs. Sets can be easily purchased and are a good way to start growing, however they can be expensive if you want to grow a large amount.

I have always started my own from seed in early March. I grow them in sets of 4 plants that way I can grow more in a small space. Seeds take a long time to germinate so if you decide to plant directly into your garden make sure you clearly mark the area.

Botanical Family: Amaryllis, onion family

Soil pH of 5.6-6.5.

Watering- Water regularly once a day at the base of the plants with drip irrigation. If the temperature goes over 28°C, water twice a day.

Fertilizer. 10N-10P-10K according to instructions above.

Seeding info for your onions:

Seed Spacing – 10-14 cm apart 1.2 cm deep

Germinate in soil temperature of 21 - 24 °C

Days to Maturity - 100-150 days

Planting Times - Sow indoors in early March; transplant at 4-8 weeks.

Planting Instruction - Sow 5 seeds in each cell (72 cell tray)1.2 cm deep. Maintain uniform moisture. Seeds will take a long time to germinate, up to 4 weeks. Limit height of transplants to 6-10 cm tall, cut with scissors to stay upright. Transplant the seedlings in a moist growing media.

Companion Planting

Positive affect: beet, cabbage, carrot, lettuce, potato, tomato

Negative affect: bean, pea

Watering - During early stages they require an abundance of water. Cut off the water once tops begin to dry out.

Care During Growth:

Make sure the place has space between them to allow for the development of the bulb.

Weeding- Keep well weeded by hand or use of recommended organic herbicide.

Disease

Back mold Fungus *Aspergillus niger.*

Botrytis leaf blight Fungus *Botrytis squamosa.*

Bulb mites Arachnid *Rhizoglyphus spp.*

Downy mildew Fungus *Peronospora destructor*.

Fusarium basal plate rot Fungus *Fusarium oxysporum*.

Fusarium damping-off Fungus *Fusarium oxysporum.*

Insects –

Leafminers *Lyriomyza sp*

Thrips *Thrips tabaci*.

Onion fly maggot *Delia antiqua*

Lesser bulb fly *Eumerus strigatus*[1]

Harvest - As the plants mature, the tops will fall to the ground. When 25-50% of the tops fall over, pull the bulbs from the growing media. Lay the bulbs in a dry sunny place and allow them to maturity. Allow them to remain there for 2-3 days. Then cut the tops 2.5 cm above the bulbs.

---

1. *https://en.wikipedia.org/wiki/Eumerus_strigatus*

Storage - Clean the bulbs by brushing lightly or using a rag. Don't use water to wash them before storing, as the dampness will encourage bacterial growth. Don't keep any mushy or soft bulbs. This is a sign that they are contaminated. Storing a contaminated bulb with healthy bulbs will cause the disease to spread. Bulbs can be store in mesh bags.

If refrigeration is available keep them above 0°C, but not above 7°C. In this manner, onions should keep for 3-8 months. Otherwise, store whole onions in a cool dry place. If stored properly onions will keep for several months.

Nutritionally, onions provide very little. They have no A, D or B12 vitamins. They do have small amounts of dietary fiber, sugar, vitamin C, calcium, and magnesium.

Pak Choi (Chinese Cabbage)

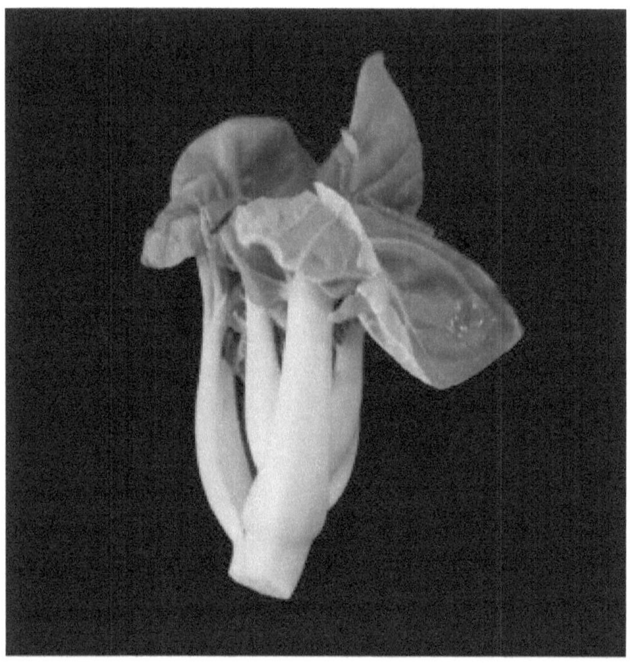

Pak choi is a shallow-rooted crop and requires frequent watering. Apply light irrigations to avoid leaching. Summer growth require a shading net. Do not over fertilize as large amounts of nitrogen have been correlated to increase in bacterial soft rots.

Botanical Family: Brassicaceae, cabbage family

Soil pH: 6.5-7.0

Watering- Water regularly once a day at the base of the plants with drip irrigation. If the temperature goes over 28°C, water twice a day.

Fertilizer. 10N-10P-10K according to instructions above.

Sow your Pak Choi seeds in seed trays for transplanting, or directly where they are to grow, and space the plants 30-40 cm apart. Protect the seedlings from slugs and snails. Grow in full sun and provide plenty of water.

Harvesting, storing and marketing

Pak choi is usually harvested by hand, cut at the base 35-55 days after sowing. Always pick pak choi when leaves are fresh and crisp, and before the outer leaves turn yellow. Remove any dead or damaged leaves, trim the base flush with the first petiole and wash the plant. Harvest during a cooler part of the day. Market prices are highest for green, turgid produce.

Pak choi is extremely susceptible to wilting. However, at 1°C and relative humidity greater than 85 per cent, white-stemmed pak choi can be stored for 7-14 days and the green-stemmed pak choi for 12-20 days. Modified atmosphere packaging can increase shelf life even further.

Pak Choi plants can be harvested as salad plants after about 30 days. After 45 days, the plants will have developed a heart and from then on can be harvested for adding to stir fries. You can treat Pak Choi as a "cut and come again" crop or use the whole plant in one go, whichever you prefer.

There is a choice of which types of Pak Choi to grow. There is even a mini variety, try Pak Choi Bonsai[1]. Pak Choi Choko[2] can tolerate the warmer weather and is a good choice for growing in summer. Pak Choi Joi Choi[3] is a dark green variety that is cold tolerant

---

1. http://www.kingsseeds.co.nz/shop/Vegetables/Vegetable+Groups/Brassica+Family/
   Pak+choi+-+Bok+choi.html

2. http://www.kingsseeds.co.nz/shop/Vegetables/Vegetable+Groups/Brassica+Family/
   Pak+choi+-+Bok+choi.html

Insects

Aphids

Cabbage Loopers

Cutworms

Whitefly

Flea Beetles

Army Worms

Grasshoppers

Snails and slugs

Diseases

Anthracnose

Downy mildew

Fusarium Wilt

Damping off

Stem Canker

Bacterial soft rot

Turnip Mosaic Virus

Nutritionally, Pak Choi is a good source of both Vitamin A and Vitamin C. Just 100g of Pak Choi will give you half your daily

---

3. http://www.kingsseeds.co.nz/shop/Vegetables/Vegetable+Groups/Brassica+Family/

  Pak+choi+-+Bok+choi/Pak+Choi+Joi+Choi+F1-7955.html

requirement of Vitamin C and 84% of your daily requirement of Vitamin A.

Peas

We all love to eat fresh picked peas. They are a cool season crop that grow and mature quickly. This vegetable is easy to grow and a joy to eat. There are two types: shelling and edible pods. The shelling variety is where you open the pod and eat the green peas from inside. A snow variety have flat edible pods and are used in salads and stir fry recipes. The snap variety fills out like a shelling variety however unlike the shelling variety the pod is edible.

Botanical Family: Fabaceae, bean family

Soil pH 6.

Peas will tolerate moderate amount of acidity, but the soil should not be over rich in nitrogen.

Seed Info-

Seed Spacing – 5 cm apart and 2-4 cm deep

Peas can germinate in soil temperature of 5 – 23 C

Days to Maturity - 100-120 days

Companion Planting

Positive effect: carrot, corn, cucumber, eggplant, lettuce, radish, spinach

Negative effect: tomato, turnip

Watering- This vegetable suffers most from heat and drought. They require regular watering.

Trellising: See cucumbers for how to trellis.

Weeding - Keep weeded while plants are young.

Insects –

Thrips

Weevils

Aphids

Nematodes

Red Spider Mites

Disease

Pea wilt (Fusarium oxysporum f.

Downy mildew (Peronospora viciae)

Leaf and pod spots (Ascochyta pisi,

Mycosphaerella pinodes & Phoma medicaginis)

Botrytis, or grey mould (Botrytis cinerea)

Powdery mildew (Erysiphe pisi)

Foot and root rots (Fusarium solani)

Harvest - Shelling: pick full pods every second day to keep plants producing. Snow: pick when flat pods are 3 inch long. Snap: pick when pods are full.

Storage - Can be stored in a plastic bag in the refrigerator for up to a week.

Nutritionally, peas provide a good amount of vitamin C. Green peas are low in calories in comparison with beans, or other legumes. Green peas have many minerals such as calcium, iron, copper, zinc, and manganese, vitamin K, and close to a quarter of the daily need of in thiamin, vitamin A, and folate.

Peppers

Peppers are a warm season crop. They are divided into 3 groups: sweet, mild and hot based on their degree of hotness. This vegetable needs a lot of sun and heat to produce well. They can be seeded directly however they need a long growing season, so it is best to start them as transplants.

Botanical Family: Solanum, nightshade family.

Soil pH 6.0-8.0

Seed Info-

Seed Spacing – 30-35 cm apart

Germinate in soil temperature

of 24 – 28 C

Days to Maturity - 60–80 days

Planting Instruction - Transplants need to be well watered.

Companion Planting

- Positive affect: basil, carrot, onion, oregano, marjoram
- Negative affect: fennel

Watering - Need to have regular watering during early stage of growth, once the plant is established less water is needed.

Weeding - Keep weeded while plants are small.

Insects –

Red spider mite,

Aphids,

Cutworms.

Tomato Hornworms.

Pepper Weevils.

Root-Knot Nematodes

Flea Beetle.

Disease

Blossom end rot

Bacterial spot

Phytophthora Root Rot.

Verticillium Wilt.

Rhizoctonia Root Rot.

Bacterial Leaf Spot.

Cercospora Leaf Spot.

Powdery Mildew.

Phytophthora Pod Rot.

Black Mold.

Viruses

TEV

TMV

PeMV

CMV

Harvest -When fruit is firm it is ready to pick; fruit will ripen further to red or yellow skin; once they are harvested more fruit will form. The time to pick peppers to achieve the highest sugar levels, is when they turn color. Take a pepper that is in the middle of changing from green to red. It will have blotches of brown. First taste a green portion of pepper, then red and finally brown. The brown will not only have the best sugar levels, it will have the best sugar: acid ratio to give the best taste.

Storage - Store in a tightly sealed plastic bag in the warmer part of the refrigerator. They will last 1-2 weeks. Do not wash if storing fresh. They can be preserved by drying, pickling or canning.

Peppers provide good nutrition and are low in calories. Nutritionally, peppers provide (depending on variety and color) are excellent sources of vitamins A and C, potassium, folic acid, and fiber. The red peppers have almost 11 times more beta-carotene and 1.5 times more vitamin C than green bell peppers.

Radishes

Radishes are the fastest growing vegetable in the garden. They are direct seeded and germinate quickly. You will need to thin the young plants, so plants are 2.4 cm apart.

They mature in approximately 30 days and do not last long once they mature so harvest them quickly. Succession planting every few weeks lets you harvest all season.

This plant will do well in a container, just make sure they are watered well, do not let them dry out.

Botanical Family: *Brassicaceae,* mustard family.

Companion Planting

Positive: bean cabbage, cauliflower, cucumber, lettuce, pea

Negative: squash, tomato

.

Soil pH: 6.0-7.0

Planting info for Radishes

Seed Info

Seed Spacing – 4-6 cm apart and 2 cm deep

Days to Maturity - 25-60 days

Planting Instruction - Form a shallow trench with a hoe; drop in seeds (2 seeds every 2") then cover and firm soil down. Water well. Thin to every 2 inches. Need to grow quickly; need lots of water.

Watering - This vegetable needs a great quantity of water. They will become bitter or hot tasting if they do not get enough water.

Fertilizer: 16N-20P-0K

Weeding– organic weed control-

Disease.

Alternaria blight Fungus Alternaria spp.

Black root Fungus Aphanomyces raphari.

Clubroot Fungus Plasmodiophora brassicae.

Downy mildew Fungus Peronospora parasitica.

Fusarium wilt (Yellows) Fungus Fusarium

oxysporum.

Scab Bacteria Streptomyces scabies.

Wirestem (Damping-off) Fungus Rhizoctonia

solan

Insects

Cutworms.

Flea beetles.

Aphids.

Harlequin bugs.

Cabbage loopers.

Harvest - Pull the whole plant when they are ½" or more in diameter.

Storage - Store in refrigerator for up to a week.

Nutritionally, radishes provide folate, fiber, riboflavin, and potassium. They also have decent amounts of copper, vitamin B6, magnesium, manganese, and calcium. Radishes contain fiber in the form of indigestible carbohydrates.

Scallions (Green Onions)

Scallions often called green onions or bunching onions are easily grown. Start your transplants sowing 5-10 seeds per transplant container. Transplant them out together and in a few weeks, you have an instant bunch of onions for your salad or other recipes.

Botanical Family: *Amaryllis*, onion family

Soil pH of 5.8-6.4.

Likes cool temperatures

Seed Info

Seed Spacing – 10-15 cm apart

Germinate in soil temperature of

21 - 24 C

Days to Maturity - 100-150 days

Transplant at 4-8 weeks.

Planting Instruction - Sow 10 seeds in each cell (24 cell transplant tray) 1.5 cm deep. Maintain uniform moisture. Put a handful of compost in the hole while transplanting.

Companion Planting

Positive effects: beet, cabbage, carrot, lettuce,

potato, tomato

Negative effects: bean, pea

Watering- During early stages require an abundance of water.

Fertilizer: Any 1N:2P:2K ratio will work

Weeding– Keep the area weed-free.

Disease

Back mold Fungus *Aspergillus niger.*

Botrytis leaf blight Fungus *Botrytis squamosa.*

Bulb mites Arachnid *Rhizoglyphus spp.*

Downy mildew Fungus *Peronospora destructor*.

Fusarium basal plate rot Fungus *Fusarium oxysporum*.

Fusarium damping-off Fungus *Fusarium oxysporum.*

Insects–

Leafminers *Lyriomyza sp*

Thrips *Thrips tabaci.*

Onion fly maggot *Delia antiqua*

Lesser bulb fly *Eumerus strigatus*

Harvest - Plant can be pulled when green tops are 8-12 inches tall. They will be in bunch of 10 or so.

Storage - Do not store well. Keep in plastic bag in the refrigerator.

Nutritionally, scallions provide very little. They have no A, D or B12 vitamins. They do have small amounts of dietary fiber, sugar, vitamin C, calcium, and magnesium.

Spinach

Spinach is a fairly easy vegetable to grow, however you need a rich soil that contains a lot of organic matter. This vegetable grows better is cool weather, so if you plan to grow during the summer months plant it between taller growing vegetables so it will get some shade.

Botanical Family: *Amaranthaceae*

Soil pH 6.2-6.9.

Companion Planting

Positive: cabbage, celery, eggplant, onion, pea, strawberry

Negative: none

Seed Info -

Seed Spacing – 15 cm apart

Germinate in soil temperature of 5 – 20 C

Days to Maturity - 40 – 60 days

Planting Times- Sow indoors early April to mid-July; transplant at 4 weeks. Succession plantings every 2 weeks. Can direct seed but will need to be thinned to every 15 cm.

Watering - Regular watering by thoroughly soaking plants late in the day; water more often during the hottest part of summer.

Fertilizer: Use any fertilizer with the following two ratios: 3-1-2 or 4-1-2 **nitrogen**, phosphorus and potassium

Weeding - Keep weeded.

Insects –

Caterpillars. A variety of caterpillar species infest spinach plants.

Wireworms. Wireworms are the larval form of beetles, known as click beetles.

Crown Mites are pests of spinach plants which are nearly invisible to the naked eye.

Slugs and snails

Aphids. ...

Leafminers.

Disease

Bacterial leaf spot Pseudomonas syringae pv.

spinacea

Bacterial soft rot Erwinia carotovora

Witches'-broom Rickettsia-

like organism

Anthracnose

Fusarium

Damping off

Downy Mildew

Harvest - Harvest outer leaves before sun hits them or spray them before cutting. Cut individual leaves with a scissors or sharp knife. If the center of the plant is left the plant will grow back and can be cut again. Cut the whole plant at the 2nd or 3rd cutting if the weather is warm. Plant goes to seed if the weather is hot.

Storage - Place moist leaves in plastic bags then place in refrigerator and they will keep up to a week.

Nutritionally, spinach is a good source of vitamin K, vitamin A, manganese, folate, magnesium, iron, copper, vitamin B2, vitamin B6, vitamin E, calcium, potassium and vitamin C. Spinach has a good amount of dietary fiber, phosphorus, vitamin B1, zinc, protein and choline.

Squash - Winter and Summer

Squash is a warm season crop and comes in a variety of shapes and sizes. Some common winter varieties are pumpkins, butternut, buttercup, spaghetti, and dumpling. Some summer varieties are patty pan, green and yellow zucchini. They do well during long, hot, humid days and warm nights. When planting your vegetable garden plan a large amount of space for this vegetable. They have sprawling vines with large leaves shaped like a palm leaf. There are some dwarf or bush varieties if you have limited space. They have both the female and male flowers; they need bees to pollinate for fruit to form.

Botanical Family – *Cucurbitaceae*, Melons,

squashes, cucumbers

Soil pH 5.5-6.6.

Seed Info-

Seed Spacing -50 cm apart

Germinate in soil temperature of

25 – 35 C

Days to Maturity - 70-105 days

Planting Instruction - Set out bush like plants (ie: zucchini) in regular beds. Vine types need to be trellised or they will cover a large area to cover. Vines can be pinched back after they get some length on them to stop wandering.

Companion Planting

Positive effects: bean, corn, mint, nasturtium, radish

Negative effects: potato for summer squash

Watering - Require regular watering.

Fertilizer: 5N:10P:10K

Weeding- Keep weeded while plants are small.

Insects–

Aphids

Cucumber beetle
Pickleworms
Squash Vine Borer
Squash Bugs
Spider Mites

Squash beetle

Disease

Bacterial Wilt.

Powdery Mildew. ...

Gummy Stem Blight. ...

Anthracnose. ...

Alternaria Leaf Spot. ...

Cercospora Leaf Spot. ...

Fusarium Wilt. ...

Viruses

CMV

SqMV

ZYMV

Harvest-

Summer (zucchini, and similar varieties): fruit grows quickly so harvest every few days. When fruit is 8 inches long cut with a knife 2 inches from the end of the fruit; do not twist off or you can harm the plant.

Winter: harvest when skin is hard; if your thumbnail does not leave a mark on the skin they are ready to harvest. Cure by leaving fruit in the sun for a few days; turn every few hours and cover if left out at night.

Storage - Store in a cool dry place that has good circulation. Stored too warm it will develop dark spots and wilted skins. If properly stored they will store for several months. Once cured place them in a single layer on a shelf in a cool place. Wiping plants every few weeks with an oily cloth prevents mold. Check them regularly for signs of softening.

Nutritionally, squash has antioxidants such as zeaxanthin, carotenes, and lutein in its skin. Summer squash has more potassium than a banana by weight. It's rich in B-complex vitamins, folate, B6, B1, B2, B3, and choline, as well as minerals like zinc and magnesium. It also contains small amounts of the essential minerals such as iron, manganese, and phosphorus.

Swiss Chard

Swiss chard is probably the most popular leafy vegetable after spinach for cooking. It is easy to grow and will do well during the spring and summer months. This vegetable can be direct seeded or transplanted. I like to transplant this vegetable that way there is no thinning to be done on your hands and knees in the garden. The more you pick off the outer leaves the more the plant will continue to grow. This vegetable will also do well in containers.

Botanical Family: *Amaranth*

Soil pH: 6.5-6.8.

Seed Info

Seed Spacing – 20 cm apart

Germinate in soil temperature of 10 - 30 C

Days to Maturity - 60 days

Likes cool temperatures.

Companion Planting

cabbage, celery, eggplant, onion, pea, strawberry

Watering - Water regularly at the base of the plants. If you sprinkle the large leaves may impede water from getting to the soil.

Bolting is when a flower stalk develops, cut it off. Unlike other greens, Bolting doesn't mean the end of the season. Chard will continue to make edible leaves all year long.

Fertilizer: 12N-0P-0K

Weeding - Keep weeded while plants are small.

Insects

Cabbage worms,

Aphids,

Flea beetle,

Leaf miners

Slugs and snails

grasshoppers

Disease

Cercospora leaf spot

Downy mildew

CMV

Harvest - You can cut the whole plant but usually harvested by cutting outer leaves when they are 6" or more in length. Leaves can be cut several times during the season. Must be cooled quickly by getting them into refrigerator as soon as possible.

Storage - Is best stored in a sealed plastic bag or container in the refrigerator. It is best to use within a few days as it loses nutrients after the first few days.

Nutritionally, Swiss chard provides an excellent source of vitamins K, A, and C. It is a good source of magnesium, potassium, iron, and dietary fiber.

Tomatoes

Tomatoes need a good soil starter mix, warmth, sunshine and care.

Botanical Family: *Solanum,* nightshade family.

Soil pH: 6.0-6.8.

Seed Info:

Seed Spacing – 30-40 cm apart

Germinate in soil temperature of 24 – 32 C

Days to Maturity average 70 – 100 days

Planting: - Sow a seed in each cell of your seedling tray. Germinate the seeds in a warm (25-28 °C) place. Transplant seedlings when they are 15-20 cm tall with at least 4 leaves. Don't let them get too tall and skinny before transplanting.

Planting Instruction: – Water your growth media before transplanting. Make holes in your growth medium every 30-40 cm.

Insert a plantlet into each hole. Then press down on both sides of the plantlet to improve the contact between the root mass and the growth media. If there are air pockets due to poor contact then the plantlet will develop slower. Add a handful of compost to the hole when transplanting.

Fertilizer: Tomatoes grow well with several different fertilizer ratios. any ratio of 1:1:1, 5:10:5, 5:10:10

Companion Planting

Positive effects: asparagus, basil, cabbage, carrot, onion, parsley, peas, sage

Negative effects: fennel, potato

Care during the Season

Greenhouse tomatoes need almost daily care. Once the plants are 18 cm tall you must attach them to a string hanging from a support wire from above. The string should be tied with a loose loop around the support wire. This allows the string to be moved up and down the row. The easiest way is to insert the bottom of the string deep into the growth media or attach it to something solid that is not at a great angle. Wrap the seedling around the string.

Remove all side branches. This needs to be down every 2-3 days. The side branches reduce the energy of the plant. The best way to remove the side branches is with a sharp knife. Don't yank the side branches off as it often causes a strip of the outer tissue to be torn off, opening the plant to infection.

Many cluster varieties need to have the end of the cluster (last 2-3 fruits) removed to ensure more uniform ripening and large sized fruit.

Red arrows point to side branches that need to be removed and the blue arrows point to the black string wrapped around the main stem of the plant.

Watering – Keep the plants watered regularly. Irregular watering and lack of calcium can cause blossom end rot. If the fruit is splitting it is a sign, they are not getting enough water.

Weeding - Keep weeded while plants are small.

Insects –

Aphids

Colorado Potato Beetle.

Cutworms.

Hornworms

Leaf miners

Nematodes

Slugs and snails

Stink Bugs.

Spider Mites.

White flies

Disease

Alternaria stem canker.

Early blight.

Damping off.

Blossom End rot

Fusarium crown and root rot.

Fusarium wilt.

Gray leaf spot.

Gray mold.

Leaf mold.

Tobacco mosaic virus (TMV)

Tomato mosaic virus (ToMV)

Tomato spotted wilt virus (TSWV)

Pepino mosaic virus (PepMV)

Cucumber mosaic virus (CMV)

Harvest - Pick fruits that firm and red, yellow or any other color the variety may be. Green fruit can be harvested and will ripen inside your house.

Storage - Store ripe fruit on the counter or shelf. Firm green fruit can be wrapped individually in paper and stored in a cool dark place. Check regularly for ripened fruit. Do not wash before storing.

Nutritionally, tomatoes are the major dietary source of the antioxidant[1] lycopene, which has been linked to many health benefits, including reduced risk of heart disease and cancer. They are also a great source of vitamin C, potassium, folate and vitamin K.

---

1. https://authoritynutrition.com/antioxidants-explained/

Turnips and Rutabaga

Turnips have a small white round root with a thin skin. Rutabagas have a big yellow root often called a winter turnip. These vegetables can be seeded in the spring to be harvested early in the season or in mid-July for a fall harvest. There is no need to harvest all the roots at one time as they will remain tender in the soil for up to 2 months. Rutabagas will improve in flavor after a frost as well. Start harvesting when the roots are the size of a golf ball. The greens are very nutritious so use them as well for salads or steaming.

Botanical Family: *Brassicaeae*/Mustard Family

Companion Planting

Positive: bean, peas

Soil pH: 6.0-6.5

Info on planting Turnips:

Seed Spacing – 25 cm apart and 1.5 cm deep

Germinate at soil temperature of 15 – 30 C

Days to Maturity - 30-60 days

Planting Instruction - Hand seed. Water well once seeded. Will require thinning once they start to grow.

Watering - Regular thorough soaking.

Fertilizer: 10-10-10, or 10-20-10 or 16-16-8:

Weeding- Keep weeded while plants are small.

Insects

Aphids

Cabbage root maggot

Flea beetle,

Weevils

Disease

Anthracnose (*Colletotrichum higginisianum*)

Cercospora leaf spot (*Cercospora brassicicola*)

White spot (*Pseudocercosporella capsellae*)

Downy mildew (*Peronospora parasitica*)

Bacterial leaf spot (*Pseudomonas maculicola*)

Club root disease (*Plasmodiophora brassicae*[1])

Rhizoctonia rot (*Rhizoctonia solani*)

---

1. *https://en.wikipedia.org/wiki/Plasmodiophora*

TuMV

TuYMV

Harvest - Leaf: Cut greens when young and tender. Add to salad mix. Root: pull the whole plant when the root is the size of a golf ball or more in diameter.

Storage - Tops need to be used quickly. Roots will store for several weeks in the refrigerator or in a cool area packed in sand, sawdust or peat moss.

Nutritionally, turnips provide a great source of minerals, antioxidants, and dietary fiber. They are a low-calorie vegetable – a 100 gram is only 28 calories. Turnip has immune-boosting vitamin C. Turnips have been found to help several colon dysfunctions. They have also been found to reduce blood pressure.

REFERENCES

Albert, S. How to Grow Mustard. 2009. http://www.harvesttotable.com/2009/02/how_to_grow_mustard.

Aphid Taxa Hierarchy. 2017,

http://aphid.speciesfile.org/Common/basic/
Taxa.aspx?TaxonNameID=115945

Bacci, L.; Battista, P.; Cardarelli, M.; Carmassi, G.; Rouphael, Y.; Incrocci, L.; Malorgio, F.; Pardossi, A.; Rapi, B.; Colla, G. Modelling Evapotranspiration of Container Crops for Irrigation Scheduling. In Evapotranspiration—From Measurements to Agricultural and Environmental Applications; Gerosa, G., Ed.; IntechOpen Limited: London, UK, 2011; pp. 263–282. ISBN 978-953-307-512-9. Nikolaou, G.,

Beauchemin M. Scientists Are Using Sunflowers To Clean Up Nuclear Radiation. May 2016 http://gardencollage.com/new-noteworthy/innovation/scientists-using-sunflowers-clean-nuclear-radiation.

Doubrava, N. et. al. 2016 Cucumber, Squash, Melon & Other Cucurbit Diseases. Clemson Cooperative Extension

http://www.clemson.edu/extension/hgic/pests/plant_pests/veg_fruit/hgic2206.html.

Herb Planting Guide - Fedco Seeds[1]

---

1. https://www.google.co.il/
url?sa=t&rct=j&q=&esrc=s&source=web&cd=1&cad=rja&uact=8&ved=0ahUKEwjIydS9lcz
TAhULKcAKHfL5DBMQFgglMAA&url=https%3A%2F%2Fwww.fedcoseeds.com%2Fseeds
%2Fherb_chart.htm&usg=AFQjCNEK9ly8mUUhq0ZE90dBThMytGNQEQ&sig2=N46Qi
wimdzGrF2pXHlGw0Q

https://www.fedcoseeds.com/seeds/herb_chart.htm

Fulcher, F.A.; Buxton, J.W.; Geneve, R.L. Developing a physiological-based, on-demand irrigation system for container production. Sci. Hortic. 2012, 138, 221–226.

Grant, B.L. 2017 What Is An Indicator Plant: Using A Plant Indicator To Improve Garden Health. https://www.gardeningknowhow.com/garden-how-to/info/plant-indicator-info.htm

Grant, B.L. 2017 How Do Aphids Help Ants: Controlling Aphids and Ants On Plants. https://www.gardeningknowhow.com/plant-problems/pests/insects/controlling-aphids-and-ants.htm.

Grant, B.L. How To Grow Anise. https://www.gardeningknowhow.com/edible/herbs/anise/growing-anise.htm

Green, R., L. Erickson, R. Govindaraju, and P. Kalita, 1997, Modeling the Effects of Vegetation on Heavy Metals Containment: 12th Conference on Hazardous Waste Research, Kansas City, Missouri, pp. 476-487.

Grossman, M. R., & Endres, A. B. (2000). Regulation of genetically modified organisms in the European Union. American Behavioral Scientist, 44(3), 378-434.

How to use tensiometers? 2009.

http://agriculture.vic.gov.au/agriculture/horticulture/vegetables/vegetable-growing-and-management/how-to-use-tensiometers

Kaller, B. Using Plants to Clean Contaminated Soil

Aug. 2014 http://www.resilience.org/stories/2014-08-11/using-plants-to-clean-contaminated-soil

Lambert, M., Leven, B.A. and Green, R.M. New Methods of Cleaning Up Heavy Metal in Soils and Water. Environmental Science and Technology Briefs for Citizens. http://www.engg.ksu.edu/HSRC/Tosc/metals.pdf

Lambert, M., G. Pierzynski, L. Erickson, and J. Schnoor, 1997, Remediation of Lead-, Zinc-, and Cadmium-Contaminated Soils: in R. Hester and R. Harrison, Contaminated Land and Its Reclamation, the Royal Society of Chemistry, Cambridge, p.91 – 102.

Lanini, W.T. Organic Herbicides - Do They Work?

http://ucnfanews.ucanr.edu/Articles/Feature_Stories/Organic_Herbicdes_-_Do_They_Work/

Mateljan, G. May 2017. The World's Healthiest Vegetables: Cucumbers.   http://www.whfoods.com/genpage.php?tname=foodspice&dbid=42

Marigolds, Tomatoes & Spider Mites. http://homeguides.sfgate.com/marigolds-tomatoes-spider-mites-51810.html

Matson, P.A. Parton, W.J., Power, A. G. & Swift, M. J. (1997) Agricultural Intensification and Ecosystem Properties. Science. Vol. 277, Issue 5325, pp. 504-509

Meronuck, R.A., Hardman, L.L., Lamey, H. A. 2017 Edible bean disease and disorder identification. University of Minnesota Extension

Mierzejewski, K.2017. Planting Melons: Information on Growing Melons. https://www.gardeningknowhow.com/edible/fruits/melons/growing-melons.htm

Read more at Gardening Know How: Planting Melons: Information on Growing Melons https://www.gardeningknowhow.com/edible/fruits/melons/growing-melons.htm

http://www.extension.umn.edu/garden/yard-garden/vegetables/
edible-bean-disease-and-disorder-identification/

Moore, S D., Kirkman[2], W., Richards, G.I. . Stephen[3], P.R. 2015. The *Cryptophlebia Leucotreta* Granulovirus—10 Years of Commercial Field Use. Viruses[4].; 7(3): 1284–1312.

Nelson, C.H. 2001 Risk Perception, Behavior, and Consumer Response to Genetically Modified Organisms.*Toward Understanding American and European Public Reaction* American Behavioral Scientist. Vol.44 issue 8.

Neocleous, D., Katsoulas, N. and Kittas, C. Irrigation of Greenhouse Crops.   2019.   file:///C:/AgroSearch/Cannabis%20Editing/ horticulturae-05-00007-v2.pdf

Petrick JS[5], Frierdich GE[6], Carleton SM[7], Kessenich CR[8], Silvanovich A[9], Zhang Y[10], Koch MS[11](2016). Corn rootworm-active RNA DvSnf7: Repeat dose oral toxicology assessment in support of human

2. https://www.ncbi.nlm.nih.gov/
   pubmed/?term=Kirkman%20W%5BAuthor%5D&cauthor=true&cauthor_uid=25809025

3. https://www.ncbi.nlm.nih.gov/
   pubmed/?term=Stephen%20PR%5BAuthor%5D&cauthor=true&cauthor_uid=25809025

4. https://www.ncbi.nlm.nih.gov/pmc/articles/PMC4379571/

5. https://www.ncbi.nlm.nih.gov/
   pubmed/?term=Petrick%20JS%5BAuthor%5D&cauthor=true&cauthor_uid=27436086

6. https://www.ncbi.nlm.nih.gov/
   pubmed/?term=Frierdich%20GE%5BAuthor%5D&cauthor=true&cauthor_uid=27436086

7. https://www.ncbi.nlm.nih.gov/
   pubmed/?term=Carleton%20SM%5BAuthor%5D&cauthor=true&cauthor_uid=27436086

8. https://www.ncbi.nlm.nih.gov/
   pubmed/?term=Kessenich%20CR%5BAuthor%5D&cauthor=true&cauthor_uid=27436086

9. https://www.ncbi.nlm.nih.gov/
   pubmed/?term=Silvanovich%20A%5BAuthor%5D&cauthor=true&cauthor_uid=27436086

and mammalian safety. Regul Toxicol Pharmacol.[12] 2016 Nov;81:57-68. doi: 10.1016/j.yrtph.2016.07.009. Epub 2016 Jul 18.

Philips, S. 1989. Greenhouse Gardening. Hamlyn Publishing Group Ltd. London, England.

Celery. Plant Village. https://www.plantvillage.org/en/topics/celery

Pleasant, B. 2011. All About Growing Melons

http://www.motherearthnews.com/organic-gardening/fruits/growing-melons-zm0z11zkon

Roades, H. 2017. Tips on Growing Celery

https://www.gardeningknowhow.com/edible/vegetables/celery/tips-on-how-to-grow-celery.htm

Sahling, L. 2015 Genetically Engineered Foods – Scientific Miracles or Minefields? CoBank Knowledge Exchange. http://www.cobank.com/Knowledge-Exchange/~/media/Files/Unsearchable%20Files/Knowledge%20Exchange/2015/KEReport-GMOs-Apr2015.pdf

Schnoor, J., 1997, Phytoremediation: Groundwater Remediation Technologies Analysis Center Technology Evaluation Report TE-98-01, 37.

Sizing the Greenhouse Water System. 2019

---

10. https://www.ncbi.nlm.nih.gov/
   pubmed/?term=Zhang%20Y%5BAuthor%5D&cauthor=true&cauthor_uid=27436086

11. https://www.ncbi.nlm.nih.gov/
   pubmed/?term=Koch%20MS%5BAuthor%5D&cauthor=true&cauthor_uid=27436086

12. https://www.ncbi.nlm.nih.gov/
   pubmed?term=long-term%20effects%20of%20eating%20gm%20crops&cmd=correctspelling

https://ag.umass.edu/greenhouse-floriculture/fact-sheets/sizing-greenhouse-water-system

Shaffer, G. 2019. Organic Herbicides. https://extension.sdstate.edu/organic-herbicides

Stephens, J. M. (2009). Celeriac — *Apium graveolens* L. var.rapaceum (Mill.) Gaud. Beaup. University of Florida IFAS Extension. Available at: http://edis.ifas.ufl.edu/pdffiles/MV/...[13]. [Accessed 10 November 14].

Stillwell, S. 2015. List of Organic Pesticides

http://www.livestrong.com/article/167183-ways-to-prevent-hazardous-waste.

Trisha 2016. Modifications of Stem (Explained with Diagram)

http://www.biologydiscussion.com/plants/modifications-of-stem-explained-with-diagram/6222

Wood, P., 1997, Remediation Methods for Contaminated Sites: in R. Hester and R. Harrison, Contaminated Land and Its Reclamation, the Royal Society of Chemistry, Cambridge, p. 47 71. U.S. Environmental Protection Agency.

USDA Yearbook. 1961.Seeds. Dept. of Agriculture, USA.

(US EPA), 1998, A Citizen's Guide to Phytoremediation, Office of Solid Waste and Emergency Response (5102G) EPA 542-F-98- 001 August 1998. US EPA, 2000, Introduction to Phytoremediation, National Risk Management Research Laboratory, Office of Research and Development, EPA/600/R-99/107, February

Broccoli Pests and Diseases

---

13. http://edis.ifas.ufl.edu/pdffiles/MV/MV04300.pdf

http://www.no-dig-vegetablegarden.com/broccoli-pests-and-diseases.html

Van Iersel, M., Burnett, S. and Kim, J. 2010.

How much water do your plants really need?

https://www.greenhousemag.com/article/gmpro-0310-water-plants-automating-irrigation/

Walker, N.W. (1936) Fresh Vegetable and Fruit Juices. Norwalk Press, Prescott, Arizona. pg. 47.

Wallister, J. 2014. Nine Diseases Killing your Eggplant.

Hobby Farms. http://www.hobbyfarms.com/9-diseases-killing-your-eggplant-4/

West, B. & Drost, D. (2010). Celery in the Garden. Utah State University Cooperative Extension. Available at: https://extension.usu.edu/files/publi.... [Accessed 10 November 14].

Williamson, J. 2015. Cucumber, Squash, Melon & Other Cucurbit Insect Pests. Clemson Cooperative Extension.

http://www.clemson.edu/extension/hgic/pests/plant_pests/veg_fruit/hgic2207.html